✦ Straight Talk about Death for Teenagers ✦

Straight Talk about Death for Teenagers

How to Cope with Losing Someone You Love

◆

Earl A. Grollman

BEACON PRESS ◆ BOSTON

Beacon Press
25 Beacon Street
Boston, Massachusetts 02108-2892

Beacon Press books
are published under the auspices of
the Unitarian Universalist Association of
Congregations.

"The Elephant in the Room" by Terry Kettering,
Bereavement (October 1989), reprinted by permission
of Bereavement Publishing, Inc., 8133 Telegraph
Drive, Colorado Springs, Colorado 80920.

09 08 07 06 05 13 12 11 10 9

Text design by Lisa Diercks

Library of Congress Cataloging-in-Publication Data

Grollman, Earl A.
  Straight talk about death for teenagers: how to cope with losing
someone you love / Earl A. Grollman.
      p.   cm.
  Summary: Suggests ways to deal with the grief and other emotions
felt after the death of a loved one and to discover how to go on living.
    ISBN 0-8070-2500-3. — ISBN 0-8070-2501-1 (pbk.)
    1. Bereavement in adolescence.   2. Grief in adolescence.
[1. Death.   2. Grief.]   I. Title.
BF724.3.G73G76   1993
155.9'37'0835—dc20   92-34540
                                                                CIP
                                                                 AC

To

NETTA
DAVID, JOANNE, JENNIFER, AND ERIC
SHARON, THANIEL, AARON, AND SAM
JONATHAN, MARSHA, REBECCA, AND ADAM

FOR THE MIRACLE OF LIFE AND LOVE
THAT UNITES ONE GENERATION TO THE OTHER

CONTENTS

Acknowledgments

I owe so much to so many people that any listing will leave out someone. Therefore, I will first thank those whose names are not mentioned, but should have been. Thank you for your encouragement and advice.

A deep, resounding appreciation for those who have read the manuscript and whose valuable insights are incorporated in the text: Mary Anne Schreder, Beverly Chappell, John D. Morgan, Deanna Edwards, Sally M. Featherstone, Joanne V. Rovee, Donna Schurman, Sharon Grollman, Netta L. Grollman, Jennifer R. Grollman, Laurie Richardson, Elanna Chodin, Shirley Chodin, Nancy Evdoxadis, and Gerri L. Sweder.

I would be remiss not to mention Susan Rosenburg, who helped prepare this book.

To Wendy Strothman, my editor and director of Beacon Press, many thanks for skillful guidance and support. How proud I am to be associated with Beacon Press, the publisher of a dozen of my previous books.

Words cannot express my heartfelt gratitude to the hundreds of bereaved young people who have openly and willingly shared themselves at a very painful time in their lives. Their tragedies and triumphs are woven into the fabric of this book.

All these people have been gifts in my life. I feel honored to have received their counsel, and I continue to be grateful for what I have learned from each of them.

INTRODUCTION

I have spoken to thousands of students in middle schools and high schools about dealing with death. These students often ask, "How come when someone dies, people forget about us? Everyone is trying to help the little kids or the parents, but what about us? Don't we count?"

I dedicate this book to you, the forgotten mourners. May you better understand your emotions, manage your grief more wisely, and discover that although someone you love has died, you still want to go on *living*.

The Elephant in the Room

There's an elephant in the room.
It is large and squatting, so it is hard to get
     around it.
Yet we squeeze by with, "How are you" and "I'm fine."
And a thousand other forms
     of trivial chatter.
We talk about the weather.
We talk about work.
We talk about everything—
     except the elephant in the room.

There's an elephant in the room.
We all know it is there.
We are thinking about the elephant
     as we talk together.
It is constantly on our minds.
For you see, it is a very big
     elephant.
It has hurt us all.
But we do not talk about the
     elephant in the room.
Oh please, say her name.
Oh please, say "Barbara" again.

Oh please, let's talk about the
     elephant in the room.
For if we talk about her death,
Perhaps we can talk about her life?
Can I say "Barbara" to you and not

have you look away?
For if I cannot, then you are leaving
   me
Alone . . .
In a room . . .
With an elephant . . .

—*Terry Kettering*

♦   *Part One*   ♦

The First Days after a Death:

What You May Feel

You face many losses during your life.

Loss is something you feel when you become separated from someone or something you care a lot about.

Perhaps one of your friends has grown distant.
Or perhaps your family has moved to a new neighbor-hood.

But life continues with new friends in new surroundings . . . eventually.

Ending is the price you pay for beginning.

Death is a different kind of loss.

With death, there are no new beginnings, only a sad, sad ending.

Just as you are struggling to make some sense of your life, you are now facing the death of a loved one.

It's the hardest loss of all—that ultimate, unalterable loss.

Nothing has prepared you for this.

With death, you may experience many crushing losses all at once:

- loss of trust: if a special person could die, couldn't it happen to you or a member of your family?
- loss of security: What will happen to you now?
- loss of faith: How could God ever let this happen?
- loss of opportunity: There is so much more you might have done together.
- loss of dreams: Life will never be the same.
- loss of identity: You thought you were starting to know yourself. Now you have more doubts than ever before.
- loss of purpose: The road ahead is so uncertain.

✦ Grief ✦

You are going through a grieving process.

Grief is not a disorder, a disease, or a sign of weakness.
It is an emotional, physical, and spiritual necessity, the price you pay for love.
The only cure for grief is to grieve.

Buried grief can cause a war within you. It is like a time bomb ticking underground.
When it does explode, it can do a great deal of damage.

The pain may be so powerful that you can't believe anyone on earth could possibly understand it.
When people ask, "Where does it hurt?" you want to shout, "EVERYWHERE!"

Some teenagers say that it's like having a tooth removed without novocaine.
A poet from the nineteenth century, Henrich Heine, called grief "a toothache of the heart."

But really, there are no accurate descriptions.

When will you feel better?
No one can give you that answer.
There is no timetable for how long you will hurt.
You can't measure grief in terms of a calendar.

There is no correct way to grieve and no way to know
how long you will grieve.

Grief does not travel along a straight line and then fade
away and disappear.
There is no cookbook for grief. There are no recipes.
You may have contradictory feelings at the same
moment.
The experience of loss is uncharted territory.

If only you could get your hands on some magic pills to
achieve a miracle cure.
There are no such pills.
There is no easy way out.

But remember this:
You will eventually feel better.

Maybe those who share your loss *seem* to be getting better. Why not you? Why is it *only* you who feels such despair?

Don't compare your suffering with that of others. You don't know their pain. They don't know yours.

Discover your own needs and don't let others direct your grief.

Allow yourself to heal at your own pace.

The grieving process depends on many personal factors.

Your relationship with the person who died:
It's like a wound on a body. Some cuts are mere scratches and heal rapidly; others are very deep, and need a long time to heal.
You will be affected by how close you were to the person who died and how deeply your life will be altered.

Your coping strategies:
How you have handled emotional distress in the past.

Your supports:
Whether you have friends or family with whom you can openly share your anguish, who won't tell you how to feel, and who won't say that everything's okay when it isn't.

Circumstances surrounding the death:
A suicide, an AIDS death, a fatal crash caused by a drunk driver, a death after a lingering illness—each produces a different grief reaction.
Your age, religious beliefs, and sex can influence the way you cope.

The intense feelings of grief are scary.
Yet they are real.
Though teenagers experience death in different ways,
there are some common landmarks along the journey of
grief.
Knowing about the process will help you understand
some of the normal reactions.

There is nothing wrong with you if you have some of the
feelings described on the following pages.
Or if you don't.
Give yourself permission to feel the way you are feeling.
Feelings keep changing.

Sometimes you may not even know what you feel.

✦ *Dazed* ✦

Is this really happening?
You're not ready for this.
You feel no pain, no anger, nothing.
You stop listening, stop hearing, and feel like you have
stopped breathing.
You are numb.

A teacher calls on you in class but you don't hear your
name.
Like a robot, you are functioning mechanically. You are
on automatic pilot—a spectator in your own life.
Your body is not connected to your mind.

Numbness helps you work through the necessary details of death.
You shut down your emotional system so you won't suffer the overload.

You require a cushion of time before the reality of loss crashes in upon you.
Emily Dickinson called this shock "the hour of lead."

It's part of the grieving process.

✦ *Disbelief* ✦

You pick up the telephone to call that special person.
You talk about your loved one in the present tense as if
he or she were still alive.
You wake up in the morning forgetting for a moment
that a tragic death has occurred.

It's not happening. It must be a mistake.
This must be a horrible dream—a nightmare.

But it isn't.

When life seems unbearable, disbelief intervenes.
It's natural to close your eyes to what is hurtful.
It protects you from the ordeal.
Fleeting moments of pretending are much needed shelter from your torment.

Disbelief can last for a few hours, a few weeks, or maybe even a few months.
It gives your emotions time to catch up with what your mind has told you.

Eventually, you must face the truth.

Your loved one is dead.

✦ *Anger* ✦

As awareness of the truth sets in, you may feel cheated, abandoned.
"Why me?"

You may be angry at:
- your friends, for saying the wrong things, or worse, friends who say nothing
- the medical community, for not doing more to save your loved one
- God, for letting this happen
- your family, for not giving you the support that you need
- the person whose carelessness caused the accident
- yourself—for feeling the way you do.

Anger feels like fire.
Let it burn itself out. Otherwise it will burn you:
  • in physical symptoms
      tiredness, headaches, digestive problems, or even
      the same symptoms that caused the death of your
      loved one
  • in loss of friends
      withdrawal that creates emotional distance, pre-
      venting you from being close to anyone
  • in feeling out of control
      lashing out at the world—making others hurt just
      as you have been hurt; lashing out at yourself.

Pain is there. You can't wish it away.
To deny your anger is also to deny the possibility of
healing.

Try to take a break by:
- going on a walk
- shooting some hoops
- screaming in private places, like in a shower or in the woods
- jogging around the neighborhood
- beating a pillow with a tennis racquet
- listening to favorite music
- or whatever brings some relief.

One of the most important ways of dealing with rage is trying to *forgive* yourself and others.

Note: *Forgive* contains the word *give*.

You *give* yourself the opportunity to place behind you those past agonies that diminish your strength and vigor.

You *give* yourself new energies to move on to meet new challenges.

You *give* yourself permission to live in an unfair, disappointing world.

Forgiveness offers a very powerful way to pull yourself out of the negative spiral of bitterness and hard feelings.

✦ Envy ✦

When you see a family having fun together, you may
think: "Why do *they* get to be so happy?"
Other kids may have families and friendships that are
still intact.

Your jealousy is a normal reaction to loss.
Others have what you have lost.

You may even become envious of the person who died.
In death one suddenly becomes all-perfect and all-wise.
You may feel threatened because you can't possibly com-
pete with these praiseworthy virtues.

Try not to make comparisons.
Just be yourself.

As Theodore Roosevelt said,
  "Do what you can,
   With what you have,
   With where you are."

You may feel that you're losing control.
- How can you get through the day?
- What if your grades drop?
- What if you get kicked off the team?
- What if you have to move?
- Who will take care of you?

Your life is one big uncertainty. Too much that you have counted on is slipping away.

You may wonder:
Will you ever be normal again?

It's difficult to get hold of yourself when your mind is a jumble.

    You can't concentrate on the simplest routine task.

    You are so tense that you just can't sit still in one place.

    You feel helpless, hopeless, disorganized.

    You want to run away, anywhere.

Emotional swings are part of the grieving process.
Your inner resources are stretched to the limit.

In time, you will gain greater control of yourself.

✦ *Relief* ✦

One kind of feeling that may surprise you is relief.

Perhaps the special person suffered intensely and now
the agony is over.
Or the person who has died was often mean or abusive,
or someone with whom you had terrible arguments.
Or he or she depended upon you so much that you're
relieved to know that your responsibility is over.

Waves of relief come and go.

These emotions are natural.

✦ *Loneliness* ✦

No one understands exactly how you feel.
Your friends are busy with their own lives.
Your parents or siblings may be wrapped up in their own grief.
And now your loved one is no longer here to share your life.

You feel a quiet, dull ache.
You are so alone.

Being *alone* doesn't always mean being *lonely*.
There are times when you may like being by yourself.
  It's peaceful and quiet.
  You're not being bugged by someone.
  You like your own company.

Alone becomes *loneliness* only when the separation makes you feel sad and dejected.

What can you do with your loneliness?

Use your time alone to think through where you are now and what you might realistically expect for the future. Understand that, even though no one can ever replace that special person, there are people in this world who will need you as much as you need them.

Recall the wisdom of the serenity prayer: "God, grant me the serenity to accept the things I cannot change; courage to change the things I can; and wisdom to know the difference."

When you are bereaved, you become susceptible to physical complaints and illnesses. It's your body's reaction to the tragedy in your life.

Maybe you:

- collapse in bed, and then can't fall asleep
- sleep more than ever but are still tired when you wake up
- are so filled with grief that you can't possibly eat; or, maybe, that you can't stop eating
- feel a constant emptiness in the pit of your stomach
- are frequently nauseous and feel like vomiting
- have pounding headaches
- feel dizzy, lightheaded, almost giddy
- find it hard to breathe
- have sensations of choking with a tightness in your throat
- are afraid you have a serious illness.

Physical symptoms may come periodically.

These symptoms may be experienced alone or in combination.
They vary in degree and intensity.

Whatever the cause, your pain is not imagined.
The agonizing period following the death of a loved one triggers the suppression of the immune system.
It is estimated that 75 percent of routine doctor's visits are for stress-related disorders or illnesses.

There is probably no crisis more stressful than the death of someone you love.

When you act as if everything is normal, a voice inside you may scream, "Am I losing my mind?"

You may do things like:
- getting lost on your way to school
- hearing voices or footsteps
- trying to call your loved one on the telephone
- talking out loud to the person who died
- seeing your loved one while walking in the mall or other places
- dreaming that you are going to visit your loved one
- forgetting your own name.

Are you having a nervous breakdown?

No.

Understand that most grieving people have similar symptoms.

When absence becomes the greatest presence,
you may transform the past into the present.
Since the death, all you can think about is your loved
one and the events surrounding his or her last living
moments.
By wishing and daydreaming, you attempt to bring the
person magically back to life.

But that doesn't make you crazy.
These are normal responses to death.

Forgive yourself when you are not as reliable or responsible as you once were.

Just remember that these strange actions and thoughts are temporary.

They fade and disappear as you continue your journey through the grieving process.

In time, it will get easier, even if you hurt sometimes. You will be able to remember your loved one without so much emotional turmoil.
You will go on to a happier and more fulfilling life.

It's hopeless.
You don't think you can bear the deep aching in your
body another minute.
Your nerves are on fire.

School has no purpose.
You withdraw from friends.
Maybe you can't stop crying, or you can't cry at all.
The slightest effort leaves you exhausted.

You are torn apart.

Depression can be disabling when you feel worthless, powerless, helpless, and unprotected.

Grief says, "How can I go on?"
Depression cries, "Why go on?"
Grief says, "Will I ever laugh again?"
Depression cries, "There is no laughter."

Depression has been described as anger turned inward.

Depression is not a weakness.
It's part of saying goodbye to someone you care about.

Be careful. Some people get stuck in depression for months and even years.

Just as it is darkest before dawn, your grief may seem endless just before it begins to lift.

It has been said: "Don't look back too often unless you want to walk in that direction."

✦ *Regrets* ✦

Grief is often filled with feelings of guilt:
If only . . . I had known she was suicidal.
  What if . . . I had insisted that he go to a better
    hospital?
      I should not have . . . let her drive the car after
        she'd had a few beers.
          I wish I could have . . . told him how much
            I really love him.

You think about all the things you should or shouldn't
have said or done.

If only you could turn the clock back.

But you can't.

There are no real answers to the question "Why?"

Philosophers have explored this question since the be-
ginning of time.
Still no one has completely solved the mystery of death.
The question "Why?" is unanswerable.
Yet you will probably continue to search for an answer.

You might experience survivor's guilt—feeling guilty for
simply being alive.
Or you may feel guilty for daring to laugh or to enjoy
yourself so soon after the death.
Or you might even convince yourself that your loved one
deliberately died in order to get away from you.

Blaming yourself and others won't bring him or her back
to life.
You don't solve problems with "if onlys."

Guilt may eat away at your very insides.
You keep remembering the times you weren't as kind
and caring and loving as you might have been.

Think about it—you can't be close to someone without
ever hurting her or him.
We all have done or said things we later regretted.

When you recall some of those things you should have
. . . could have . . . might have done, try to revive the
memories of things you *did* do or say that brought happiness to that special person.

No, you can't change the past. But you can avoid making
the same mistakes in the future.

No one is ever blameless in life.
Making mistakes is human.
When you face the past and let it go, you give the present the chance it deserves.

✦ *Part Two* ✦

Who Died and How:

Advice for Special Relationships

and Circumstances

Special Relationships

Grief is the process of separating from meaningful relationships such as the one you have with a
  • grandparent
  • parent
  • sibling
  • friend.

How well you knew the person who died, and how
much you depended on him or her, will deeply affect
your grieving process.

An old joke reads:
Question: "Why is there a special relationship between grandparents and grandchildren?"
Answer: "They have a common enemy—the parent."

There is often a special attachment between grandparent and grandchild.
Some grandparents help to raise their grandchildren.
Some provide the biggest laps for comforting.
Some are especially warm and attentive, with lots of quality time to give.
They may make few demands and give many gifts.

When a grandparent dies, you may feel sad for many reasons.

You miss someone you love.

Family gatherings will never be the same.

It may be the first time that you are confronting death and witnessing the grief of those closest to you.

Of course, not all memories are pleasant.

You may have been embarrassed when a grandparent talked too loudly in front of your friends.

You may have been impolite when you felt a grandparent was too critical of you.

You may have shown your anger when a grandparent took a parent's side rather than yours during a family argument.

Know that people of *all* ages have frustrations with each other.

How you feel when a grandparent dies will depend upon the closeness of your relationship.
If you really didn't know a grandparent well, if he or she lived far away or seldom visited, the impact of death may be slight. The more your grandparent touched your life, the deeper the sorrow you will feel.

Your grief will also be different from the grief that your parents are feeling.
Their memories and attachments are not the same.

Mourn in your own way.

People may say to you: "You're so lucky. Your grand-parent lived a long life."
But at this moment you don't feel lucky.

Whatever your grandparent's age, there is a gaping wound in your life when she or he dies.

Life changes forever when a parent dies.
Your parents made your life possible.
In part, they are responsible for who you are.
Their attitudes and behavior help shape your view of the
world.

When a parent dies, your sense of security is torn apart.
Your family will never be the same again.
You will never be the same.

You may spend the rest of your life looking for your
"lost" parent in your relationships with others.

If both of your parents have died, your journey through grief will be especially painful and complex.

It is important to know where you will be living and with whom.

Usually a close relative will guide you through this difficult time.

Participate as much as possible in the crucial decisions concerning your life.

It's your future!

You may be faced with accepting new responsibilities such as shopping, cooking, cleaning, taking care of a younger sibling, getting an after-school job.
Life was hectic enough with homework, music, sports, drama practice—and now this.

How can you balance work and pain without suffering from stress overload?
Discuss with your family the details of how you will be able to find time for yourself.

Take care of yourself the best that you can.

You may feel guilty after a parent dies, especially if you hadn't been getting along.

Maybe you felt that your parent was trying to "run" your life, treating you like a child.

Perhaps you had argued or fought.

You are now filled with so many regrets.

How could you have acted that way?

Stormy periods between teenagers and parents are natural.
So many changes are taking place in your life, your mind, your body.

Pressures can be overwhelming:
- living up to expectations at school
- getting along with friends and family
- finding some independence while you are still dependent on your parents.

You hardly know who you are from one day to the other.

There are no perfect relationships, especially during this time.
Try to remember the *happy* moments you did spend together—those fond memories that you will cherish.

There may be other family members who pull away from you.
They may be so engrossed in their own grief that they can't pay attention to you.

Maybe it's the wrong moment. Try again.
Later they may be more receptive.
Tell them what you need.
If they can't listen, write them a letter.
Very often family members want to share feelings but, mistakenly, try to protect you with silence.
Tell them it's okay to talk about sad thoughts.
All of you must come to grips with the change in your lives.
All of you need to recover.

Dare to talk openly, even cry together.
When words fail, hold each other.

You need each other more now than ever before.

Young people aren't supposed to die. They are expected to live long and happy lives.
How, then, could this happen?

You may receive little or no support from the adults in your life.
Your parents may be the focus of everyone's attention. Neighbors meet you coming home from school and ask how your mom or dad is doing.
Don't they know that you, too, are suffering?

You may recall the arguments and fights you had with your sister or brother and wonder if this is how you are being punished.

You might feel cheated that you no longer have a brother or sister.
Someone asks, "How many brothers or sisters are in your family?"
How are you supposed to answer? If you are now the only child, are you still a brother or sister? Part of your identity has been wiped away.

If your sibling was older than you, you may mourn the loss of a role model and protector.
If closer in age, you may mourn the loss of a companion and competitor.
If younger, you may mourn the loss of someone you took care of, perhaps someone who looked up to you, and someone who was sometimes a pest.

Since one child has died, your parents may become afraid that something may happen to you as well.
You may feel smothered by their overprotectiveness.
They may see danger signs everywhere they look.
They keep track of when you go out and with whom.
You come home a minute late and they're terrified.
They imagine every possible catastrophe.

Understand their anxiety.
Discuss their fears.
Try to work out your need for reasonable freedom even in their uncertain world.

Some may unfairly compare you to the sibling who died. "She did so well in school." (Are you now expected to become a better student?)

"He was a great athlete." (Are you a failure if you don't make the team?)

Some brothers or sisters unconsciously take on the mannerisms and interests of their dead sibling.

But just as you will never take the place of the sister or brother who died,

NO ONE CAN TAKE YOUR PLACE.

Each person is unique.

You have your own personality.

Just be you.

You may now want to become closer to your other family members.
They, perhaps more than anyone, will understand what the loss means to you.

Know that others have experienced the death of a brother or sister.
They, too, had to struggle through feelings like yours.
They have survived.

You will too.

✦ *Death of a Friend* ✦

Welcome to Earth. The death rate is 100 percent.

Of course, everyone dies. You have probably tried to imagine how you would react when death struck someone you cared deeply about.
You may have anticipated the deaths of older members of your family.

But not someone your age.
NOT A GOOD FRIEND.

It's almost as devastating as the death of a family member.

Sometimes it is worse.

Everyone expects you to mourn for family members. But when a friend dies, teenagers are often left alone to deal with their pain.

Adults may even say, "Why are you taking it so hard? It's not like someone in your family has died."

You may be afraid that you will "break down."

Many people bottle up their emotions and are ashamed to show their feelings.

Consequently, you may act as if nothing happened.
After all, time heals. Doesn't it?
So you wait it out.
With the passing of the days you'll reach that magical moment when you will be "whole" again.

Not true.

Time does not automatically heal your pain.
It's your willingness to touch your pain—to accept it, to work with it, to understand your change of moods and behavior, and then to begin to reorganize your life.

Healing happens as you allow feelings to happen.

Time does not completely heal a broken heart; it only teaches you how to live with it.

A romance that ends with the death of a boyfriend or girlfriend seems especially cruel.
How can you possibly deal with such suffering?
You may hurt so much that you think you will die.

It is understandable that your pain is enormous and your emotions intense.

It takes courage to confront feelings like:

ANGER

for the injustice of the death

LONELINESS

for never being together again

REGRETS

for not always being there when your friend needed you.

After the death of a friend, you may become afraid of getting close to others.
After all, they could die, too, couldn't they?

How could you ever go through this again?

Try not to withdraw from others.
Reach out. Other friends may experience similar emotions. They may also be afraid of share feelings.

Be patient with them. They, too, are struggling.
Don't assume that others know what you need unless you tell them.

Drop over and see the family of your friend and share some of your memories.
As you relieve these experiences, you will not only help them, but yourself as well.
You might even send a personal letter.

Healing involves being willing to hurt more now in order to someday hurt less.
It is the process of going through—not over, around, or under—your pain.

Special Circumstances

The circumstances of death affect the way you respond
to your loss:

Was the death sudden, accidental?

Did she take her own life?

Did he die of AIDS?

Was she murdered or killed by a drunk driver?

Did death come after a long illness?

An important factor affecting your feelings will be the
way that special person died.

✦ Accidental Death ✦

Webster defines an accident as "an *unfortunate, unforeseen* event resulting from *carelessness* . . . or an *unavoidable* cause."

It is *unfortunate.*
One moment you are fine; the next, your world is crumbling before your very eyes.

It is *unforeseen.*
You have no forewarning; you are totally unprepared.

There may be *carelessness.*
Perhaps the death could have been avoided if someone had not been negligent.

There may be an *unavoidable* cause.
There are natural disasters such as floods and hurricanes. Who ever thought such a catastrophe would affect your future?

The impact of a sudden accidental death is profound.
The psychological term is "unexpected loss syndrome."
Survivors feel an overpowering shock because life is
taken away so quickly and they are powerless.

You think:
"It can't be true. It didn't really happen."
The assault on your emotions makes it impossible to be-
lieve and accept.
Again and again you review the circumstances before the
death.

Sudden death may bring regrets and feelings of guilt.
If only you could have been there to help.
Those haunting words again: "If only."

You may imagine the final scene over and over again.

But do not punish yourself for something that cannot be changed.

✦ Self-Inflicted Death ✦

"He had so much to live for. Why would he kill himself?"

Every death is traumatic. But it can be more so when someone you care about deliberately takes his or her life.

You may feel that you didn't love enough.
You may be so ashamed and embarrassed that you feel you have to defend yourself against the critical judgments of others.

For suicide almost always causes a greater sense of failure than a natural death.
Couldn't someone have prevented it—a family member, teacher, friend, you?

Questions, doubts, and guilt are all typical reactions of those who remain after a loved one has taken his or her life.

Since it was his or her personal decision to die, you may feel abandoned and rejected.

Didn't the person love you enough to keep on living?

You might even feel a sense of relief.

This doesn't mean you are unfeeling or didn't love the person enough.

It's okay to find some solace in knowing your loved one's torment is finally over.

In your search for cause and effect, you piece together every detail leading to the death.

The question "Why?" represents your hope of making some sense out of this senseless act.

Even though a self-inflicted death is painful for the living, the decision to die was not yours. Believe it!

You are only in charge of your own destiny.

You cannot control the lives of others no matter how much you love them.

You probably did the best you could with what you had and what you knew at the time.

✦ *AIDS* ✦

Like suicide, AIDS is called a "stigmatic death."

Since AIDS is often associated with homosexuality, promiscuity, or drug use, friends and family members often feel humiliated and disgraced.

They may feel crushed.

Your special person has died and you don't need to bear the additional burdens of other people's prejudice and intolerance.

Feelings of loss do not begin at the time of death; they start when the diagnosis of HIV positive is first made. At this early stage you may experience feelings of shock, betrayal, and frustration.

Later, you may also experience a sense of failure and guilt, if your loved one died alone, unattended, isolated, and in pain.

The bereaved travel a very crooked path on their unexpected journey through sorrow.

The greatest memorial you can erect to a loved one with AIDS is to effectively educate others about this disease. Knowing the facts may help you in this task:

- AIDS is an abbreviation for Acquired Immune Deficiency Syndrome, a weakness in a person's ability to fight off diseases or infections.
- AIDS is caused by a blood-borne virus that is not spread through casual contact.
- No one is immune because of their sexual preference, race, or economic class.
- Gay men and IV drug users are not the only people who contract AIDS. AIDS cases are increasing among heterosexuals now at twice the rate of that for homosexuals.

- One-fourth of the teenage population has or has had a sexually transmitted disease.
- Since the symptoms of AIDS may not appear for ten years, it is estimated that 19 percent of those with AIDS are young people in their twenties who contracted the disease as teenagers.
- Most sexually active teenagers do not use condoms. That's why it's called "suicide sex."
- Intercourse of any kind can be risky behavior even with condoms.
- Local health departments usually offer free, anonymous testing.

This deadly disease will continue to spread unless proper precautions are taken. The best defense against AIDS is information. You might wish to seek further advice from health professionals.

Society is unaccustomed to an epidemic that resists the magic of medicine.

Until there is a cure for AIDS, there is outreach. Families and friends may need extra social and emotional understanding and care.

Reach out with unconditional support.

There are also community agencies who can help turn you from fear, anger, and confusion to acceptance and readjustment.

Their motto is: "Love heals those who give and receive it."

✦ Death by Violence ✦

Death is a trauma: a complete shock to the survivors.
Death by murder or by a drunk driver ranks among the
most severe traumas.
An act by another person has destroyed part of your
future.

More and more states are charging second- and third-
degree *murder* in drunk driving deaths because driving
drunk displays extreme indifference to human life.
Someone's recklessness killed your loved one.
An automobile can be as much a weapon of destruction
as a gun or a knife.

You are caught in the tragic effect of the crash.

Murder is a particularly devastating loss to face.
The public nature of this outrage adds further
complications.
Murder involves legal procedures with attorneys, police
investigations, and maybe even a trial.
Newspapers, radio, and television reporters may turn
your loss into a media event.
It may take five to seven years for the criminal justice
system to complete all the appeals of the case.

You are not a spectator in a story on TV, but a participant
in a terrifying real-life drama.

How difficult it is to heal under these circumstances!

In many instances—in cases of both murder and of death by a drunk driver—the guilty person may not be found or sentenced.

If there is a verdict, it might appear to you too lenient. It may make you feel robbed and victimized twice: first, because your loved one's life has been needlessly taken; second, because the guilty person has not been punished enough.

It's very hard to even imagine forgiveness!

You may try to imagine how it must have been when your loved one died.
You envision the graphic details as you relive the crime.
Was there much suffering?
You feel ravaged as you picture the final horrifying scene.

If only you could stop thinking about it.
You try, but these thoughts haunt you when you are awake, and in your dreams when you sleep.

It's natural to feel hatred and bitterness, and to think of revenge.

In your rage you may secretly plan a torturous retaliation—a life for a life.

Recognize that your thoughts are normal.

Just don't act on these impulses.

Use your justifiable anger to lobby for stronger victims' rights.

It is important to find supportive people and organizations such as state victim assistance programs to help you cope with your terrifying nightmare and the slow process of recovery.

✦ *Death after an Illness* ✦

People may ask: "Why are you taking it so hard? You knew he was dying. It's not as if you didn't have any warning. Didn't you have time to prepare yourself for this?"

They don't understand.
Death almost always feels unexpected; it happens before you're ready.
No one can completely plan for death. Death makes its own plans.

Yes, you probably knew how sick your loved one was.
Yet you are still swept away by overpowering emotions.
You are numb and unprepared *even after* the long illness.
Death still comes as a surprise.

You may be confused because part of you is glad that this special person is no longer in pain.
Don't feel guilty; it's natural to feel relief when suffering has ended.

It doesn't always help when people say to you, "Thank God her suffering is over."
Your *loved one's* suffering may be over, but not *yours*.

Don't allow others—or even yourself—to deny your suffering.
Your sadness is the result of loving someone.
Would you be willing to forgo your ability to love so you would never have to hurt again?

Every love story ends in death.

◆ *Part Three* ◆

Facing Your Immediate Future

✦ *Attending the Funeral* ✦

The funeral may be an important family event that confirms the reality of death.
When the service is being planned, the bad dream becomes real.

Together you gather for emotional support.
Grief shared is grief diminished.

Facing your loss through a funeral is a significant step in your healing and recovery.

You may wish to be included in making the arrangements.

You may want to help choose the casket, or the prayers or music.

You might even want to write a poem or speak at the service.

For some, viewing the body helps them realize that their loved one has really died.

Going to the cemetery underlines the ultimate finality of your loss.

The funeral may be the beginning of your awareness of separation.

It's all right to cry.

✦ *Spirituality* ✦

Before the death of your loved one you may not have
given a lot of thought to the theological problem: "Why
do good people suffer?"
Questions about life after death may not have seemed
important.

Death often changes life's meanings.
You may now want to search for a spiritual response to
the sorrow you feel.

Many teenagers find consolation in their religious faith.
Participating in the rituals of the funeral, reading the
Scriptures, believing in a hereafter—all may bring a
sense of belonging, comfort, and hope.

You may be surprised to find yourself furious at God for allowing this to happen.
Great religious leaders, and the Bible, have asked: "My God, why have you forsaken me?"

Anger is a normal response to grief.
It's okay to be angry with God. God can take it.
The sooner you express your emotions, the more quickly you will be able to resolve them.

Some mourners may believe that God is punishing them because they didn't go regularly to services, hadn't prayed hard enough, or maybe said or did some things they're not proud of.
Don't inflict additional pain upon yourself.
Death is not a penalty for bad behavior.

ALL people die.

✦ Returning to School ✦

School may feel like a second family to you.
Most of your time is spent in class surrounded by school-mates and friends.

After the death of a loved one, you may dread returning to class.
You are frightened:
- How will your friends and teachers react?
- What if someone makes an incredibly stupid and in-sensitive remark?
- How can you study and continue to live as if nothing ever happened?
- What if you cry?

Some teenagers feel better when the class has already learned about the loss.
Perhaps a parent or family friend could inform the principal before you return to school.
Obviously, you don't want to be singled out and embarrassed.
But you won't have to go through the guessing game: "Have they heard?"

Instead of focusing on your work, you may stare aimlessly out the school window.
You have difficulty concentrating on your studies.
If grades understandably begin to slip, you may feel even more depressed and inadequate.

Some adolescents let go of their anger by acting out in class and behaving badly.
Misconduct, frequent headaches and stomachaches, and absenteeism may be signs that you should consider asking for counseling.

However, as you begin to recover, so will your school performance, as well as your relationships with your family and friends.

Special days like the anniversary of your loved one's death, birthdays, Mother's/Father's Day, Thanksgiving, Christmas, Chanukah, High Holidays, New Year's Eve, graduation, prom day, or Valentine's Day can be particularly difficult.

The first time you are not with the person you loved on a special day, you may feel like Chicken Little: "The sky is falling. The sky is falling."

Unfortunately, there are no magic formulas to remove suffering.

Avoiding pain is not an option. The question is how you will manage the pain for that day.

Planning ahead may lessen some of your despair. You need to feel less like a victim and more like a survivor.

You may decide to do things differently on this special day; like changing old routines or starting new customs. Just don't escape into loneliness.

Choose the right people to be with—those friends or relatives who will let you share your innermost feelings. You should be able to mention your loved one's name, tell favorite stories, cry, or laugh at funny memories.

Remember your loved one in a meaningful way: light a memorial candle, look through a photo album, watch home videos, write a letter to that person, compose a poem, draw a picture, or visit someone else who is alone and suffering.

◆ *Part Four* ◆

Learning to Cope

An old Chinese proverb reads, "The journey of a thousand miles starts with a single step."

The first step in coping with your grief is to accept your loss.
Of course, you know in your *mind* that the special person is dead.
You say it out loud.
Your ears listen to the words.
Yet you still may not believe it.

You may fantasize that you will see this individual again in your lifetime.

Many people have trouble saying the word DEAD.
Instead, they use phrases like "passed," "gone away,"
"departed," "expired," "left on a long journey."
It's as if the beloved is going to return.

Acceptance does not mean that you have to like what
has happened.
Instead, it is the awareness that life has changed and
that you must now respond to these new circumstances.

Reality may hurt for a while, but denial hurts even
longer.

✦ Accepting the Pain ✦

You can't heal what you don't feel.
If there is pain, it's because of a wound you can't see.
You don't help yourself by running away from your emotions and pretending that nothing has happened.

Accept and allow yourself to experience your hurt.
Try not to say: "I shouldn't feel the way I do."
Your feelings are natural and okay, even though they may be scary and painful.

Beware of those who encourage you to hide your normal feelings by telling you to "be strong."
Young men in particular are too often discouraged from grief work.
The popular term *macho* is a Spanish word meaning "aggressively masculine."
A *macho* person is someone unmoved by distress, and who doesn't show that he's hurting.

The British call it "keeping a stiff upper lip."
The Japanese name is *gaman*.
Hispanics may pride themselves on their ability to *aguantar*, to be indifferent to pain.
Whatever the language, the intent is the same:

Be brave. Be strong.
Be silent.

WRONG!
BE YOURSELF!

Strange, isn't it? We praise people for bearing their burdens quietly rather than urging them to feel their sorrow.

Unexpressed grief, like hidden anger, stays with you and takes its toll later.
That's when the macho ones may hit bottom.

Respect your feelings.
Don't carry your grief in silence.
Allow yourself to mourn and grieve for what was and what could have been.

✦ Lengthening Grief through Harmful Shortcuts: ✦ Drugs and Drinking

You may want to forget, to escape these intense feelings by sleeping.
You're so tired; yet you have difficulty dozing off at night.
There may be sleeping pills in the medicine chest.
Or your nerves are on edge.
How about tranquilizers?
Blot out your misery.
Smoke a joint.
Take cocaine or other drugs.

Drugs block out feelings and memories, but only for a brief time.
Eventually you must face your problems.

Drugs hide your natural emotions.
They interfere with the free flow of recovery.

Maybe a few beers will calm you down.
They won't; alcohol is a depressant.
When the effects wear off, you'll feel worse than before.
And alcohol or drugs can kill you.

Drugs and alcohol cannot help you escape.
Alcohol + drugs + grief = greater grief.
You can't short-circuit the grief work.

You must allow the natural healing process to take place.

You may have been involved in athletics and were physically active.

Now you get tired just walking down the school corridors.

You are exhausted, wiped out.

You may not care whether you eat or not.

Yet especially in this weakened state during mourning, your body absolutely demands nourishment and care.

Eat regularly and as nutritiously as possible.

When you notice yourself rushing and getting tense, try to slow down.
Take short breaks.

Regular exercise is important in reducing stress.
Even if you hate it, exercise helps you feel better.

Rest also helps to heal both body and mind.
You can't cheat on your health and get away with it.
Your physical condition affects your mental state.

Take responsibility for your well-being.
Have a complete check-up.
Tell the doctor about the loss in your life.
Physical disturbances usually clear up within days or weeks.

But if you continue to feel awful, don't assume the complaints are only the result of your grief.

Neglecting your health won't bring your loved one back to life.

✦ Talking ✦

In times of difficulty, silence is not golden.

You do not lighten your emotional burdens by keeping
them bottled up inside.
Your angers, frustrations, and disappointments will fes-
ter like a sore within you.
Talking gets it off your chest.
The anguish building inside you is released.

Feelings that you keep to yourself may be distorted and
feel even worse than they actually are.
The thoughts that seem so terrible when they wander
through your mind may seem different when you speak
them.
Life may not be so hopeless, after all.
When others respond to you, you learn to understand
yourself better.

Someday you will be able to talk about your loved one
without feeling so much emotional suffering.
Then you know you are beginning to heal.

Some people may have good intentions but may not be
helpful. They want to take away your pain instantly and
make it all better. Or maybe they just don't know what
else to say.

They may say:	*You may think:*
"You're so young. Don't be so upset. You have the rest of your life ahead of you."	"Don't you know I'm hurting and that I feel like I'll hurt forever?"
"Just think happy thoughts."	"Death is all I can think about, and you expect me to find happiness in that?"
"I know just how you feel."	"How can you? You don't live inside of me. You have no idea. . . ."
"Thank God he's not suffering anymore."	"Thank God? But why did God allow him to suffer in the first place?"
"Something a lot worse happened to me."	"I don't need to hear about your problems now. I have enough of my own, thank you."

You may feel more desperate and alone because of their unsolicited advice.

Try to remember that they really don't want to hurt you.

Help them by letting them understand what *you* are feeling and going through.

If you don't talk to each other, you run the risk of ending up as strangers.

If you do talk, you could be rewarded with a stronger relationship.

There are friends who will truly listen and say:

"I care about you."

"You're not alone. I'm with you."

"I remember when. . . ." and recount a memory of your loved one.

"What can I do for you now?"

"You talk . . . I'll listen."

Don't be afraid to share who you are.

✦ Crying ✦

You may have heard someone say: "I was so moved that I broke down and cried."
Think about it. Silly, isn't it? Cars break down.
People weep in order to express wordless messages of pain.

You might cry at unlikely moments in improbable places—sitting in the school cafeteria, listening to a song on the radio, reading a book, or watching a movie.
Don't apologize or feel embarrassed.
You are letting go of pent-up emotions.
Tears are not caused by weakness or cowardice or self-pity.

Some teenagers express their feelings openly.
Others feel just as deeply about their loss but are unable
or unwilling to cry.
Because someone else doesn't cry, it doesn't mean that
you shouldn't.
If someone does, it doesn't mean you should.

There is no "right" way to show feelings.
You respond with what is correct for you.

Of course, crying will not bring back that special person.
That's the reason for tears; you cry because you cannot
bring your loved one back to life.

The late president John F. Kennedy said, "There are three things that are real.
God, human tragedy, and laughter. Since we cannot understand completely the first two, we must do with the third—laughter."

Human tragedy may be so overwhelming that you must reduce it before you can put it into words.
Serious things are said in jest.
You let go of nervous tension with a joke.
You restore a sense of balance from the hurt that is threatening to swallow you.

You really "lighten up."

When you begin to have fun again with your friends, you may think, "My loved one is dead and here I am laughing. What kind of person am I?"

You can smile, laugh, and still love the person who died. Norman Cousins, in his book *Anatomy of an Illness*, said that ten minutes of laughing allowed him to sleep without pain for two hours.
Humor is gaining a reputation as the all-natural, do-it-yourself wonder drug.
It works without bad side effects.

Cry when you must; laugh when you can.

✦ *Writing* ✦

You may release your feelings by writing down your
thoughts.
A journal or scrapbook could be your safe place to get in
touch with your deepest emotions.
Journals are called "paper psychiatrists."

All you need is paper and pen.
Write whatever comes to mind.
Don't worry about spelling or punctuation.
Your thoughts and feelings are not going to be graded.
No one will read your journal unless you wish to
share it.

Pour out sadness, regrets, loneliness, and fears.

You might draw pictures of the way you feel or write a poem.

Include what you wish you had said to that special person, and what you wish you hadn't said.

Let your journal be your constant companion, releasing and rediscovering your inner self.

You may wish to tell that special person how much you miss him or her.

You might at last say goodbye.

A heavy burden will be lifted from your shoulders. When you reread what you had written days and weeks before, you'll suddenly realize how you have changed and grown.

It may be different now when you're with old friends.
No one knows quite what to say.
Do you still belong?
Just when you're going through an agonizing loss and
need your friends, you may become afraid of losing
them, too.

You can't expect your friends to know how you are feeling unless you express your needs clearly.
If you keep saying, "I'm fine," how will they know that
you need their help?
They can't read your mind.

Some people may disappoint you.
They don't know how to deal with people in grief.
Only *now* are you yourself beginning to understand the suffering of loss.
How would they?
Forgive them.

Don't isolate yourself from needed attachments.
Keep in touch with old friends; make new ones.
Death may bring surprises.
Those whom you barely know may become dear to you.

One teenager said, "I always used to shoot hoops with my friends. Yeah, we would talk, but mostly about girls and sports. And then my brother died. Everyone just pretended that everything was normal. Maybe I pretended more than they did. But, the truth was, I just felt so far away from them. And then this kid that I hardly even knew came up to me and started talking. His brother had died a few years before. We just clicked. I felt like he really cared."

There are those who may tell you to get hold of yourself.
How?
Your family is in their own private world of grief.
Who can understand what you are going through?
In many communities there are groups for bereaved
teenagers.
Some are sponsored by schools, churches, synagogues,
funeral homes, and hospitals.
Some are part of national family and community support
organizations.
Talk to your school counselor, hospital, or mental health
organization.
Don't isolate yourself. Seek out other people who have
had similar experiences.

In a grief support group you will be with young people who understand you.
They'll know what your concerns and fears are.
They've been there.

Young people explain how teenage support groups are so healing for them:

- "I don't feel embarrassed to cry here."
- "I can let go of my anger and pain without someone telling me that I shouldn't feel that way."
- "I can smile, I even laugh, without feeling guilty."
- "I don't feel like I'm so alone anymore. People can reach out to me. And I can reach out to them!"
- "I've learned to be more patient and more of a friend to myself."
- "I've learned to be more of a friend to others."
- "I know that others have been through this, and they've survived. I think I can, too."

Together you form friendships and learn how to cope as you begin to rebuild your lives.

You cannot work through such a devastating loss and not be changed.
You, who have experienced grief, are better able to understand the grief of others.

You could become a wounded healer reaching out to others in their time of need.
You could be a member of a support group, a hospital volunteer, or a peer counselor for the hot line in your community.
Reach out.
Befriend a lonely classmate.
Visit residents in a nursing home.
There are a lot of people who need your understanding and compassion.

In relating to others, you start to let go of that terrible
emptiness in your heart.
You take the focus off yourself.
You reinvest yourself in others.

Helping to carry someone else's load lightens your own.
Reaching out makes you feel needed, wanted,
important.

Love multiplies by division.

As a result of your loss, you will have more room for
other people's pain than you may ever have had before.

One teenager said:

"I knew I was getting better. I mean, at least I could concentrate at school, something that I couldn't do for months after my best friend died. But then, there was still something deep inside me, that was hurting. Maybe that hurt will never go away completely. That's what I learned when I started seeing the school psychologist. She helped me to understand that. She's also helped me to get on with my life."

You might consider meeting one-to-one with a professional counselor for understanding and support during these difficult days.

Many professionals can help you: school counselors, psychologists, psychiatrists, social workers, nurses, members of the clergy, mental health professionals, grief therapists.

Be your own true friend and be aware of danger signals.

You might seek professional help if you:
- think about suicide (Seek help immediately! Tell somebody!)
- feel stuck in your sorrow without significant emotional movement or progress
- rely on drugs or alcohol
- avoid social activities and rarely want to be with others
- are always tired
- feel like you're always racing and can never relax
- are indifferent to school and the activities that were once important to you
- take risks as if you're tempting fate
- experience physical pain or can't sleep
- feel an anger that is constantly erupting
- just can't overcome your feelings of powerlessness and sadness
- don't have anyone safe to talk to
- feel no purpose in being with anyone or doing anything
- are dealing with other major stresses at this time—a broken relationship, divorce in the family, a parent losing a job, moving to a new community.

Seeking professional help does not mean that you are mentally ill.
It is a sign of courage.
You are ready to get on with your life.

A listening ear can help you express your feelings and deal with your loss.

◆　*Part Five*　◆

Rebuilding

Your Life

✦ "Getting Over It" ✦

"When will I get over it?"

It's a question you are asking yourself.
You are grieving for the person who died.
You are grieving for the person you were before your loved one died.
You might have been energetic and fun-loving, but now you are serious and absorbed.

Your friends miss the old you.
"Don't you think it's about time you're over it?" they may ask.
It's understandable. They're concerned about you.
They want you to resolve your grief completely and quickly.
They don't understand the complex mourning process.

Some ask because they want to free themselves from further involvement in your pain.
And if you pretend that you are that "old self" again they won't need to keep giving you their encouragement and support.

You don't have to play games to make them feel more comfortable.
There is no time limit on grief.

"Getting over" the death of someone you care about is not like getting over a cold or an illness.

"Getting over it" doesn't mean that you're the exact same person you were before the tragedy.

"Getting over it" doesn't mean that you have forgotten the person who died.

An old spiritual reveals this truth:
It's so high you can't get over it.
It's so low you can't get under it.
So wide you can't get around it.
You must go *through* the door.

You don't "get over" your loss.
You go through it.

Healing takes time.
Your sadness may never completely disappear.
But with time it will erupt less often and will gradually
diminish.
Most teenagers recover slowly but surely.
Pain hurts just a little bit less with the passing of the
days.
The space between grief pangs begins to lengthen and
the pangs become less intense.

With time, your suffering is softened.

Just as you're finally feeling a little bit better, you may have low periods.

Don't panic!

Your distress is not the same as when it all started at the bitter moment of death.

Yes, you have been there before. You may be there again.

But you are healing.

There are slips and falls on the journey through grief.

Gradually go forward in your recovery.

Even if you sometimes falter and fall back, continue on again.

Passing gently through grief is the only path out of your bereavement which is lasting and healthy.

Now that your physical ties to your loved one have
ended, it can be agonizing to let go of your emotional
ties.

Some people get stuck in their grief and live only in the
past.

Think in terms of possibility rather than impossibility.
You might wish to list some of the good things in life
that still remain.

Compared to your great loss at the moment, the pluses
may seem insignificant.

But even in pain you can still envision renewed
purposes.

To go on is to admit that you cannot change the reality of
your loved one's death.
To go on is not to live a pain-free life, but to take each
day as it comes and make the most out of it.
To go on means to survive and celebrate your loved one's
life.

Pain need not last forever.
Begin to release yourself from its grip.

An open hand holds things better than a closed one.

There are mementos—pictures, letters, songs, personal items—that remind you of your special person's life. At first you may feel depressed just looking at them. Why not just throw them away?

Wait.
Walk through grief; don't run.
If the reminders are too painful because your loss is so recent, put them away for the present.
There may be a day when you will treasure them.

Your loved one would want these memories to be cherished.
Concrete images of the past can become sacred.

In addition, there may be items of clothing or jewelry that you may someday want to wear. Some teenagers say this brings them comfort, helping them feel closer to their loved one.

Tell your family what you might like as a keepsake.

The poet Kahlil Gibran wrote, "Remembrance is a form of meeting."

The life that has touched yours goes on forever.

Memories are your rainbow on drab, rainy days. Remembering can transform bitter pain into happy thoughts of a life shared.

Time cannot steal the treasures you carry in your heart. What you once enjoyed, you can never lose. All that you loved becomes a part of you.

One teenager said, "I think a lot about my special friend. Sometimes I feel sad and cry. Lately, I've begun to smile when I remember what we did together. I feel better knowing that this person is with me—only a thought away."

Now that you've encountered loss, you may see life
differently.
When someone you love dies, you confront your own
mortality.
Knowing how brief life can be might encourage you
to try to make your own life more meaningful and
enjoyable.

Now that you've encountered loss, you may be looking
more deeply into your own beliefs.
What had been significant may now appear trivial.
You may set new priorities and redefine your needs.
Growing is knowing not only where you are coming
from but what you are searching for.

Now that you've encountered loss, you may have a different understanding of the meaning of love.
You realize that to love others doesn't diminish your love
for the one who died.
Love doesn't die; people do.

Grief begins with a terrible and lonely loss.
Grief has changed you but is not destroying you.
Grief is a powerful teacher.

Do you remember reading Lewis Carroll's *Alice's Adventures in Wonderland*?

"Who are You?" said the Caterpillar. Alice replied, rather shyly, "I hardly know, Sir, just at present—at least I know who I *was* when I got up this morning, but I think I must have been changed several times since then."

How different you are now.
Nothing in life had prepared you for this tragedy.
Like Alice, you have had to make many changes to adjust to your great loss.

Take small steps and take pride in your small victories.

Grief is a process.
Recovering is *your* choice.
Grief is the price you pay for love, but you don't have to go on paying forever.

You have endured the worst kind of experience.
You will survive.

There is hope.

◆ *Part Six* ◆

In Loving Memory

✦ *Recognizing Your Feelings* ✦

These words may describe how you feel. You might share these emotions with others, write them down in your journal, or just think about what is going through your mind.

empty	encouraged	frantic
relieved	embarrassed	ignored
trapped	angry	confused
scared	peaceful	guilty
numb	bitter	uncertain
restless	happy	don't believe it
determined	outraged	exhausted
lonely	serene	peaceful

Other feelings:

I feel _____

because _____

Sharing pain helps to diminish it. Listed below are some people who might help you.

friend(s)	school counselor
parent(s)	teacher
brother(s)	neighbor
sister(s)	doctor
relative(s)	minister, priest, rabbi
other	family friend

Ask around for support groups in your school or community. Write down the name, address, and telephone number.

If you are thinking about professional help, which counselors and social agencies will help you cope with your loss?

For a list of support groups you may write to:
National Directory of Children's Grief Support Systems
c/o Dougy Center
3909 S.E. 52d Avenue
P.O. Box 86852
Portland, Oregon 97286

Completing these unfinished sentences may help you express some of your hidden, unfulfilled wishes, thoughts, and feelings.

When I now hear your name mentioned, I:

The last thing I remember I did with you was:

Since your death, my life:

I always wanted to ask you:

I miss:

I wish I had:

I wish you had:

I act differently in school, for example:

My friends don't understand that:

I'm furious that:

If only:

It's a relief that:

I find it hard to forgive:

My greatest surprise since you died is:

What scares me the most is:

When I think of you, I don't miss:

If you were living now:

What I now understand about myself is:

I have changed and grown by:

I wish that you:

What I want most is:

Wonderful recollections I'll never forget are:

Grief is a continual process. What might assist you on your journey?

talking

getting involved in school and other activities

having time alone

crying

writing down your thoughts

being with friends

eating

hugging

screaming

praying

helping others

getting further counseling

joining a support group

exercising

Now that you know what you need, what will you do about it?